A

Colony

of

Ants

A

Shrewdness

of

Apes

All animals are sorted alphabetically

A 2 – 4

B 5 – 14

C 15 – 33

D 34 – 40

E 41 – 45

F 46 – 55

G 56 – 65

H 66 – 74

I 75

J 76 – 77

K 78 – 79

L 80 – 88

M 89 – 99

N 100

O 101–105

P 106 – 118

Q 119

R 120 – 128

S 129 – 143

T 144 – 149

V 150 – 151

W 152 – 159

Y 160

Z 161

A

Herd

of

Antelope

A

Troop

of

Baboons

A

Cete

of

Badgers

A

Shoal

of

Bass

A

Colony

of

Bats

A

Sloth

of

Bears

A

Colony

of

Beavers

A

Swarm

of

Bees

A

Sounder

of

Boar

A

Gang

of

Buffalo

A

Flight

of

Butterflies

A

Caravan

of

Camels

An

Army

of

Caterpillars

A

Clowder

of

Cats

A

Destruction

of

Cats(wild)

A

Herd

of

Cattle

A

Coalition

of

Cheetahs

A

Brood

of

Chickens

A

Clattering

of

Choughs

A

Bed

of

Clams

A

Quiver

of

Cobras

A

Intrusion

of

Cockroaches

A

Rag

of

Colts

A

Covert

of

Coots

A

Kine

of

Cows

A

Band

of

Coyotes

A

Cast

of

Crabs

A

Sedge

of

Cranes

A

Float

of

Crocodiles

A

Murder

of

Crows

A

Herd

of

Deer

A

Pack

of

Dogs

A

Pod

of

Dolphins

A

Drove

of

Donkeys

A

Dule

of

Doves

A

Brace

of

Ducks

A

Fling

of

Dunlins

A

Convocation

of

Eagles

A

Parade

of

Echidnas

A

Herd

of

Elephants

A

Gang

of

Elk

A

Mob

of

Emus

A

Cast

of

Falcons

A

Business

of

Ferrets

A

Charm

of

Finches

A

School

of

Fish

A

Stand

of

Flamingos

A

Swarm

of

Flies

A

Plump

of

Fowl

A

Skulk

of

Foxes

An

Army

of

Frogs

A

Harem

of

Furseals

A

Gaggle

of

Geese

A

Tower

of

Giraffes

A

Cloud

of

Gnats

A

Herd

of

Goats

A

Charm

of

Goldfinches

A

Troubling

of

Goldfish

A

Band

of

Gorillas

A

Cloud

of

Grasshoppers

A

Leach

of

Greyhounds

A

Brace

of

Grouse

A

Down

of

Hares

A

Cast

of

Hawks

An

Array

of

Hedgehogs

A

Siege

of

Herons

A

Bloat

of

Hippopotamuses

A

Drift

of

Hogs

A

Team

of

Horses

A

Pack

of

Hounds

A

Cackle

of

Hyenas

A

Mess

of

Iguanas

A

Shadow

of

Jaguars

A

Smack

of

Jellyfish

A

Troop

of

Kangaroos

A

Kindle

of

Kittens

A

Desert

of

Lapwings

An

Ascension

of

Larks

A

Conspiracy

of

Lemurs

A

Leap

of

Leopards

A

Flock

of

Lice

A

Pride

of

Lions

A

Lounge

of

Lizards

A

Plague

of

Locust

A

Risk

of

Lobsters

A

Tiding

of

Magpies

A

Sord

of

Mallards

An

Aggregation

of

Manatees

A

Stud

of

Mares

A

Richness

of

Martens

A

Mischief

of

Mice

A

Steam

of

Minnows

A

Labor

of

Moles

A

Barrel

of

Monkeys

A

Scourge

of

Mosquitoes

A

Pack

of

Mules

A

Watch

of

Nightingales

A

Herd

of

Okapi

A

Family

of

Otters

A

Parliament

of

Owls

A

Team

of

Oxen

A

Bed

of

Oysters

A

Pandemonium

of

Parrots

A

Covey

of

Partridges

A

Muster

of

Peacocks

A

Colony

of

Penguins

A

Nest

of

Pheasants

A

Flock

of

Pigeons

A

Drift

of

Pigs

A

Paddle

of

Platypus

A

Congregations

of

Plovers

A String of Ponies

A

Prickle

of

Porcupines

A

Herd

of

Porpoises

A

Coterie

of

Prairiedogs

A

Bevy

of

Quails

A

Colony

of

Rabbits

A

Gaze

of

Raccoons

A

Colony

of

Rats

A

Rhumba

of

Rattlesnakes

An

Unkindness

of

Ravens

A

Crash

of

Rhinoceroses

A

Bevy

of

Roes

A

Building

of

Rooks

A

Hill

of

Ruffs

A

Family

of

Sardines

A

Plump

of

Seals

A

Shiver

of

Sharks

A

Drove

of

Sheep

A

Dropping

of

Sheldrake

A

Shoal

of

Shrimp

A

Stench

of

Skunks

A

Nest

of

Snakes

A

Walk

of

Snipe

A

Host

of

Sparrows

A

Dray

of

Squirrels

A

Murmuration

of

Starlings

A

Fever

of

Stingrays

A

Mustering

of

Storks

A

Bevy

of

Swans

A

Spring

of

Teal

An

Ambush

of

Tigers

A

Knot

of

Toads

A

Hover

of

Trout

A

Gang

of

Turkeys

A

Bale

of

Turtles

A

Nest

of

Vipers

A

Venue

of

Vultures

A

Pledge

of

Wasps

A

Bunch

of

Waterfowl

A

Colony

of

Weasels

A

Pod

of

Whales

A

Pack

of

Wolves

A

Wisdom

of

Wombats

A

Fall

of

Woodcocks

A

Descent

of

Woodpeckers

A

Herd

of

Yaks

A

Herd

of

Zebras

www.shoebill.com

If you have any
questions/suggestions,
please contact us at
info@shoebill.com

www.ingramcontent.com/pod-product-compliance
Lightning Source LLC
Chambersburg PA
CBHW070121100426
42744CB00010B/1892